Helping Children See Jesus

ISBN: 978-1-64104-048-8

THE RESURRECTION
Death Conquered!
New Testament Volume 13: Life of Christ Part 13

Author: Ruth B. Greiner
Illustrator: Frances H. Hertzler
Computer Graphic Artist: Ed Olson, Melody Mayer
Typesetting and Layout: Patricia Pope

© 2018 Bible Visuals International
PO Box 153, Akron, PA 17501-0153
Phone: (717) 859-1131
www.biblevisuals.org

All rights reserved. No part of this publication may be reproduced, stored in a retrieval system or transmitted in any form by any means, electronic, mechanical, photocopy, recording or otherwise, without the prior permission of the publisher, except as provided by USA copyright law.

RELATED ITEMS

To access related items (such as activities, memory verse posters and translated texts) please visit our web store at www.biblevisuals.org and enter 1013 at the top right of the web page. You may need to reduce the zoom setting to get the search box.

FREE TEXT DOWNLOAD

To obtain a FREE printable copy of the English teaching text (PDF format) under Product Format, please scroll down and select Extra–PDF Teacher Text Download. Then under Language select English before clicking the ADD TO CART button to place in your shopping cart. Other languages are available at an additional cost from the Language menu. When checking out, use coupon code XTACSV17 at checkout and click on Apply Coupon to receive the discount on the English text.

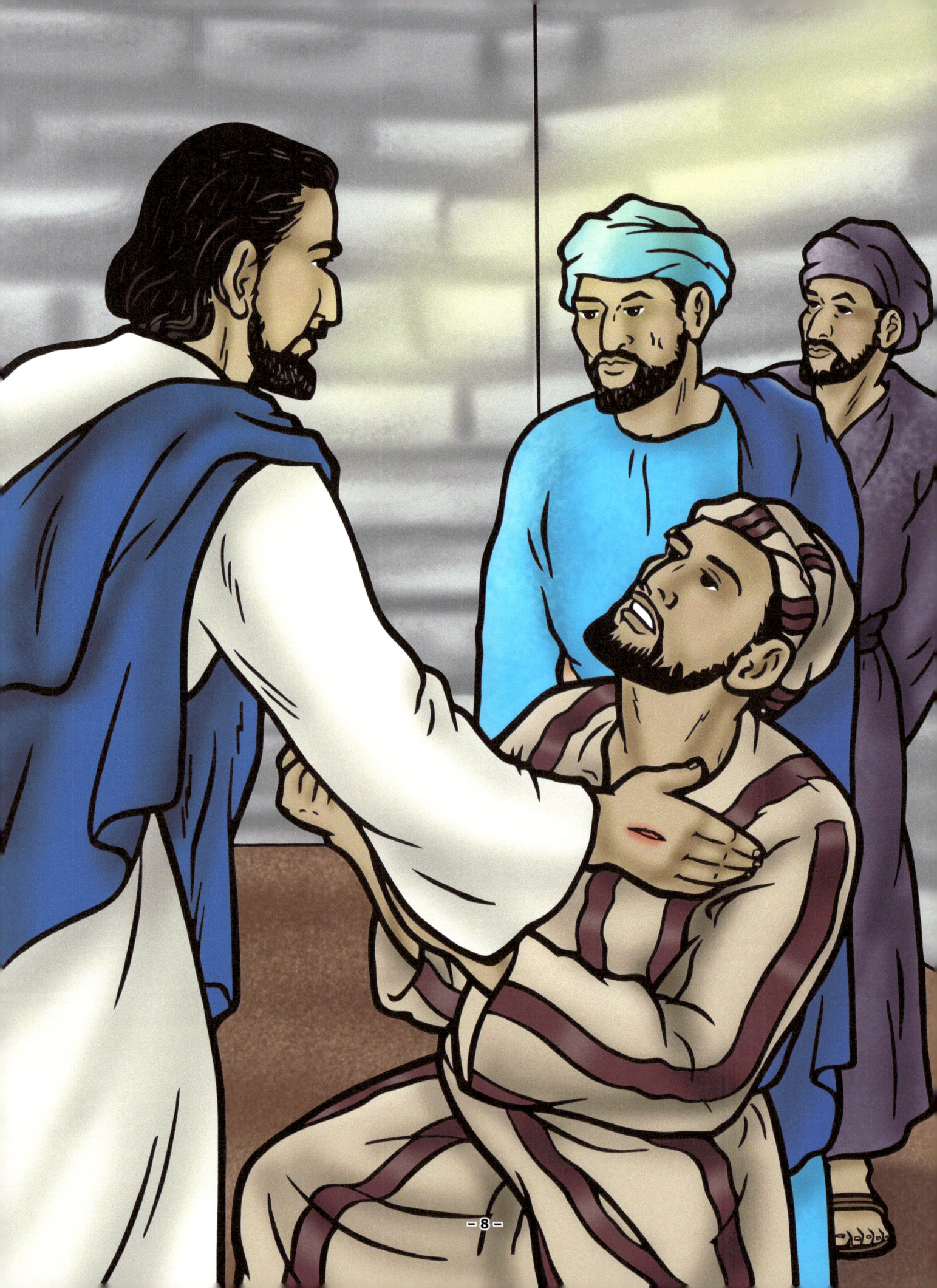

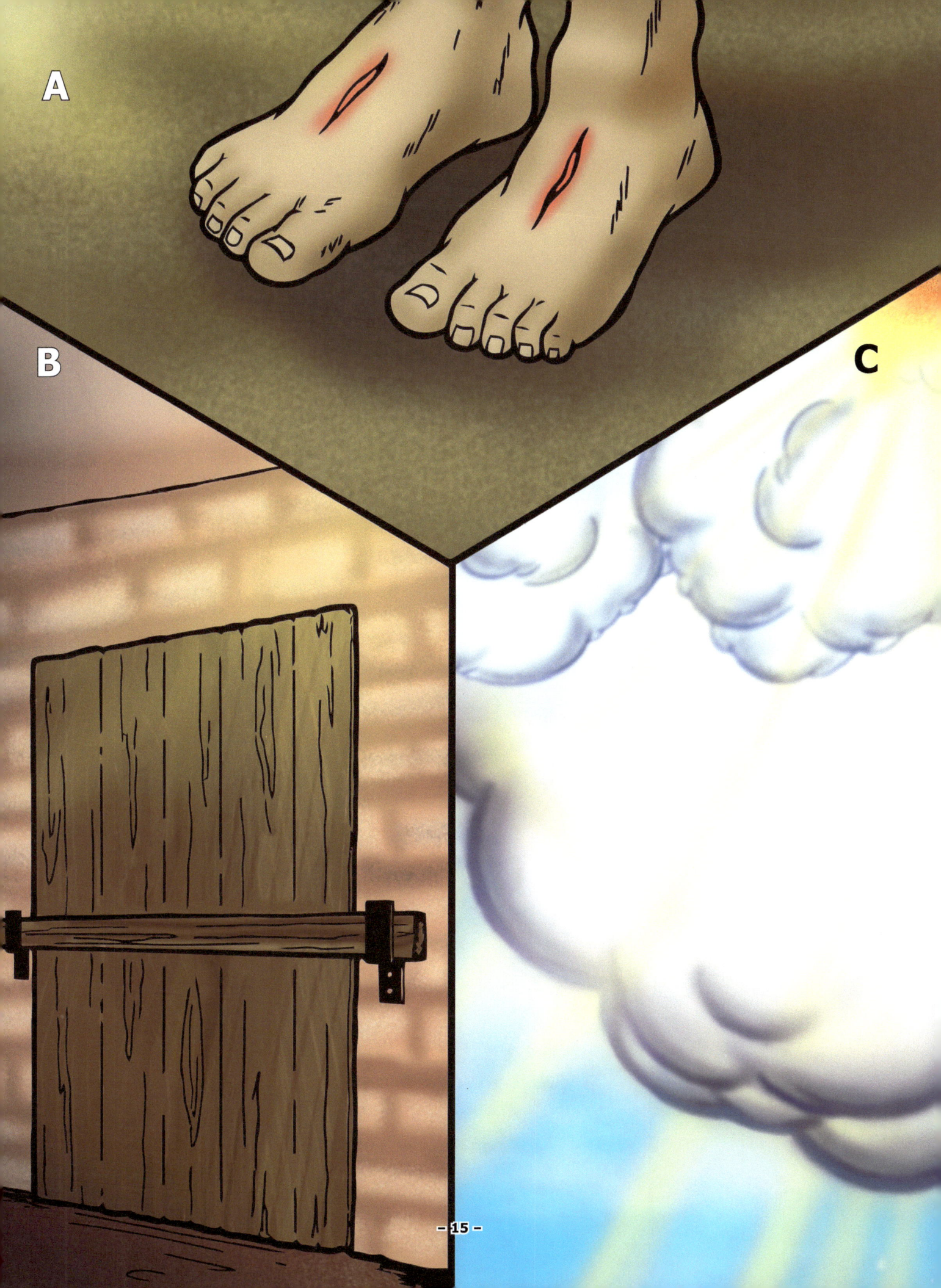

That if thou shalt confess with thy mouth the Lord Jesus, and shalt believe in thine heart that God hath raised Him from the dead, thou shalt be saved. Romans 10:9

© Bible Visuals International Inc

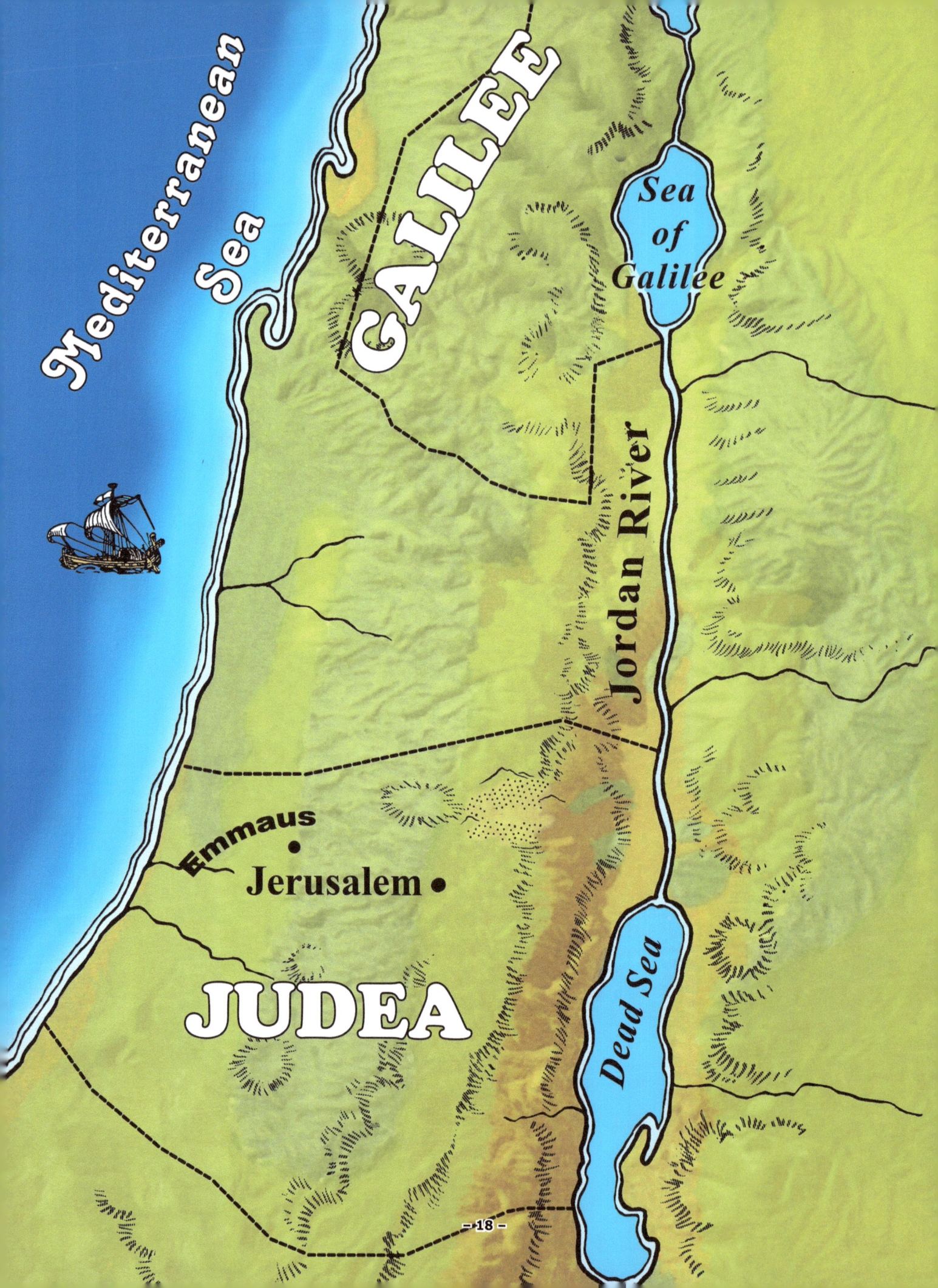

Lesson 1
JESUS LIVES!

NOTE TO THE TEACHER

The darkest day in all of history was the day the Son of God was crucified, taking upon Himself the sins of the world. The brightest day was the day of His resurrection. The doctrine of a risen Saviour is exceedingly precious. It is the cornerstone of our faith. No religion can boast of a founder who has risen from the dead. In this, the Christian faith differs from religion. By His resurrection, the Lord Jesus Christ proved He is indeed the Son of God. Even the grave could not hold Him.

It is only when we grasp something of the wonder of the resurrection that we can begin to appreciate the greatness of salvation. So teacher, ask God to help you to comprehend and relay to others the wonderful truth that we are justified by a risen Saviour and that the experience of fellowship with the risen Saviour is even more glorious than the doctrine itself.

May you "know Him, and the power of His resurrection" (Philippians 3:10). That knowledge and power should be reflected in your teaching.

Scripture to be studied: Matthew 27:57-66; 28:1-15; Mark 15:42-47; 16:1-11; Luke 23:50-56; 24:1-12; John 20:1-18

The *aim* of the lesson: To show the importance of the resurrection and the wonder of fellowship with a risen Saviour.

What your students should *know*: Jesus Christ died and rose again so all who believe in Him can be saved.

What your students should *feel*: A desire to be saved.

What your students should *do*: Believe in the Lord Jesus Christ as the Son of God and receive Him as Saviour.

Lesson outline (for the teacher's and students' notebooks):

1. Jesus' friends bury His body (Matthew 27:57-61; Luke 23:50-56).
2. Jesus' enemies demand that His tomb be guarded (Matthew 27:62-66).
3. Jesus' followers find an empty tomb (Matthew 28:1-8; Mark 16:1-8; Luke 24:1-12; John 20:1-10).
4. Jesus reveals Himself to Mary (Mark 16:9-11; John 20:11-18).

The verse to be memorized:

That if thou shalt confess with thy mouth the Lord Jesus, and shalt believe in thine heart that God hath raised Him from the dead, thou shalt be saved. (Romans 10:9)

THE LESSON

Jesus was dead. The day of His crucifixion was the darkest in all of history. Those who loved Him were filled with inexpressible sorrow. They were helpless as they watched the Son of God die on the cross.

1. JESUS' FRIENDS BURY HIS BODY
Matthew 27:57-61; Luke 23:50-56

But Joseph, a rich man from the village of Arimathea, had known one thing he could do. He had gone to the cross and carefully taken down the body of Jesus and wrapped it in white cloth.

Another man, Nicodemus, a ruler of the Jews, had also done something. He had brought about 100 pounds (45 kilos) of sweet-smelling spices and placed them with the body of Jesus in a new tomb which belonged to Joseph. The tomb was like a large cave cut out of a rock. It was almost sunset when Nicodemus and Joseph finished their loving acts.

Show Illustration #1

Then they had rolled a large, round, flat stone in front of the entrance of the tomb and left the garden.

Two women, both named Mary, had been waiting and watching while the body of Jesus was laid in the tomb. They, too, dearly loved the Son of God. When the stone to the tomb was rolled into place, the two Marys left the garden. They were sad and lonely. They knew, however, what they could do to show their love for the Lord. They would go home and prepare burial spices to be placed beside His body after the Sabbath.

Christ's disciples were deeply troubled. The death of Jesus seemed very final. Their hopes for the future had disappeared. Their Master and Teacher, the One they thought would be King, was dead and buried. They could not talk to Him. How could they continue to be His followers? They were filled with fears, doubts and dread. What would happen to them now that Jesus was dead? But they had forgotten something. They forgot what the Lord Jesus said when He was still with them: that He would rise from the dead.

2. JESUS' ENEMIES DEMAND THAT HIS TOMB BE GUARDED
Matthew 27:62-66

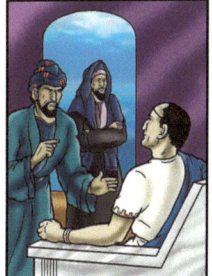

Show Illustration #2

But the enemies of Jesus had not forgotten. They were worried. Those enemies–the chief priests and Pharisees–hurried to Pilate. *What do they want this time?* Pilate wondered. *I granted their wish to crucify Jesus. Now they are back again. Why don't they leave me alone?*

One of the men explained, "O Pilate, we remember that while Jesus was still alive He said, 'After three days I will rise from the dead.' We want you to command that the tomb be guarded carefully until the third day. Otherwise His disciples will come and steal His body and say, 'He is risen from the dead.' The last mistake would be worse than the first." (The first mistake in their minds was Jesus' claim that He was the One sent by God; the second mistake, that His disciples might claim He had risen from the dead.)

Pilate listened to what the priests and Pharisees had to say. Then he answered, "You may have the guard of soldiers you want. Go and make the grave as secure as you can."

The priests and Pharisees hurried away. They made certain that the great stone was in its right place in the doorway to the tomb. The tomb was sealed by stretching a rope across the stone and fastening each end of the rope with wax. Then the official seal of Pilate was pressed into the wax. Soldiers were placed on guard. Man had done everything he could to keep the Lord Jesus in the dark tomb.

Hour after hour the soldiers kept watch in the garden to make certain that no man would break the seal.

3. JESUS' FOLLOWERS FIND AN EMPTY TOMB
Matthew 28:1-8; Mark 16:1-8; Luke 24:1-12; John 20:1-10

Show Illustration #3

The first day of the week (Sunday) was the third day after Jesus was buried. Very early that morning before the sun was up, Mary Magdalene and the other Mary and a woman named Salome left their homes carrying the spices they had prepared to place with the body of Jesus.

As they walked along the road that led to the garden, one of the women asked thoughtfully, "Who will roll the stone away from the door of the tomb when we get there?"

The other two women had no answer. They all knew that the great stone was much too heavy for them to move. (Such stones usually weighed at least 1,000 pounds–450 kilograms.) But the women went sadly on to the tomb though they had no idea how they would get inside. They probably did not know that the tomb had been sealed and guarded by soldiers.

Entering the garden at sunrise, they saw an amazing thing. The great stone had been moved aside and the tomb was empty! What did it mean? Mary Magdalene did not wait to find out. She ran to tell Peter and John. She did not know that earlier an angel had come down from Heaven, rolled the heavy stone away from the door and sat on it. The face of the angel shone like lightning and his clothing was white as snow. The soldiers were so frightened that they fell down as if they were dead. When they were finally able to get up, they had fled from the garden in terror.

Now the other Mary and Salome came closer to the open tomb. They stepped inside looking for the body of Jesus. He was not there.

Suddenly two men stood by them in shining clothes. The women were so frightened that they bowed their faces to the earth. They had never in their lives seen anything so brilliant. The men spoke: "Why are you looking in a tomb for Someone who is alive? He is not here. He is risen! Remember how He spoke to you while He was in Galilee and said: 'The Son of Man must be delivered into the hands of sinful men, and be crucified, and rise again on the third day'?"

Then the women remembered that this was exactly what Jesus had said. Why had they not thought of it before?

"He is alive! He is alive!" they cried, and ran to tell the disciples the glorious news.

By this time Mary Magdalene (who still did not know that Jesus had come back to life) found Peter and John and told them all she knew: "They have taken the Lord out of the tomb and we do not know where they have laid Him." When Peter and John heard this, they ran ahead of Mary to the tomb. John got there first and looked inside. Peter went right in and found the linen clothes and napkin that had been on the head of Jesus. It was folded and lay in a place by itself. Then John entered the tomb. And he, too, saw and believed that Jesus had risen. Joyfully, Peter and John returned to their homes.

4. JESUS REVEALS HIMSELF TO MARY
Mark 16:9-11; John 20:11-18

Meanwhile, Mary Magdalene returned to the tomb. She still did not know the wonderful news. She was crying as she stooped and looked inside. There she saw two shining white angels, one sitting at the head and one sitting at the feet of the place where Jesus had lain. The angels asked her, "Why are you crying?" She answered, "Because they have taken away my Lord and I do not know where they have laid Him."

Someone standing behind her asked the same question, "Why are you crying?" And added, "Who are you looking for?"

Show Illustration #4

Looking at Him through her tears, Mary thought He must be the gardener. "Sir," she said, "if you have taken Him away, tell me where you have put Him and I will go and get Him." She dearly loved the Lord Jesus for He had once cast seven demons out of her.

"Mary," the Man said.

Then she recognized His voice. It was not a stranger or the gardener she had been talking to. It was Jesus Himself!

"Master!" she cried as she looked into the face of the Lord she loved.

"Do not touch Me," Jesus said to her, "for I have not yet gone up to My Father. Go to My brothers and tell them that I ascend to My Father and your Father and to My God and your God."

Mary rushed to tell the disciples. "I have seen the Lord!" she exclaimed. But they could not believe it. It was too good to be true.

While the women were telling the good news that Jesus was alive, the soldiers rushed into the city to tell the chief priests what had happened. Immediately the priests and elders decided to pay the soldiers a lot of money if they would lie about what had taken place. It was agreed that the soldiers were to say that the disciples of Jesus had come and stolen the body of Jesus while they, the soldiers, had been sleeping at the tomb. (In those days a soldier could be put to death for falling asleep while he was on duty. But the chief priests promised the soldiers that if the governor heard their story about "falling asleep" they would persuade the governor not to punish them.) So the soldiers began to spread the story that the body of Jesus had been stolen from the grave. Many people believed them then. Many believe that lie today. Satan did not and does not want anyone to know that Jesus had really risen from the dead.

Do you believe that Jesus Christ is alive, that He rose from the dead? Romans 10:9 tells us "that if you will confess with your mouth the Lord Jesus, and will believe in your heart that God has raised Him from the dead, you will be saved." Are you saved? Have you "confessed" Him by telling others about Him? Write in your notebook the names of those whom you want to introduce to the Lord *this week*.

Lesson 2
APPEARANCES OF THE RISEN LORD

Scripture to be studied: Mark 16:12-13; Luke 24:13-48; John 20:19-31; 1 Corinthians 15:4-8

The *aim* of the lesson: To show that the Lord Jesus proved He was alive by His many appearances.

What your students should *know*: While we cannot see Jesus now, we can accept Him as Saviour and have the assurance we shall see Him someday.

What your students should *feel*: A desire to believe in Jesus.

What your students should *do*:
Unsaved: Believe on Jesus as the Son of God and receive Him as Saviour.
Saved: If ever they are fearful, doubtful, powerless, remember Jesus' words, "Peace be unto you."

Lesson outline (for the teacher's and students' notebooks):
1. Jesus' friends question His death (Luke 24:13-27).
2. Jesus' friends recognize Him (Mark 16:12-13; Luke 24:28-32).
3. Jesus appears to His disciples (Luke 24:33-48; John 20:19-23).
4. Thomas believes (John 20:24-29).

The verse to be memorized:

That if thou shalt confess with thy mouth the Lord Jesus, and shalt believe in thine heart that God hath raised Him from the dead, thou shalt be saved. (Romans 10:9)

NOTE TO THE TEACHER

In this lesson we learn more of the wonders of the resurrection. We see also that the risen Lord proved He was alive by His many appearances to His disciples and friends. In various ways He showed what His resurrected body was really like. He possessed a body that was recognizable by His friends. Yet He was able to do things that human beings cannot now do. In His resurrected body the Lord Jesus displayed the power of God and showed us in part what the resurrected body of the believer will be like.

Rejoice in the assurance that Christ has indeed risen from the dead! It is a truth we believe, as Mary Magdalene and the disciples believed, even though we haven't seen Christ with our eyes nor touched Him with our hands. The words of the Lord to Thomas should strengthen our faith: "Blessed are they who have not seen, and yet have believed."

THE LESSON

The news of the resurrection of Jesus Christ seemed unbelievable to those who heard of it. Yet it brought new hope to those who loved Him. Mary Magdalene was one of those who was filled with joy. She hurried into Jerusalem with the amazing news: "Jesus has risen from the dead! He is alive! I saw Him!"

The disciple John also was filled with new hope. Although he had not seen the risen Christ, he did see the empty tomb and the grave clothes lying inside it. That was enough to cause him to believe that Jesus Christ was really alive.

The news of the resurrection, however, terrified the enemies of Christ. The soldiers who guarded the tomb were no longer brave. An earthquake early in the morning and a shining angel in white clothes had frightened them so much that they had fallen as if dead. Then they fled into the city to report what had happened.

The chief priests and the other enemies of Christ were so fearful that they determined to keep the truth of the resurrection from being known. So they lied, saying the body of Jesus had been stolen from the tomb. What a foolish story that was! If the body had been stolen, the grave clothes would have been gone too. Yet, as silly as the story was, some people actually believed it!

1. JESUS' FRIENDS QUESTION HIS RESURRECTION
Luke 24:13-27

Sad to say, even some of the friends of Jesus did not think His resurrection could be true. Some reasoned that Jesus had been seen only by a few women–not by any men. They thought the women had imagined they saw Him or that they saw a vision–not the real, living Lord. The people who had not seen the risen Christ could not believe He really was alive.

On that same Sunday afternoon, two followers of Jesus (one named Cleopas) were walking from the city of Jerusalem to the little town of Emmaus, seven miles away. On any other day Cleopas and his friend would have been happy. But on this day they were troubled. They had heard strange things from men and women who saw and reported that the tomb where Jesus had been buried was now empty. Cleopas and his companion did not know what to think. How could they really believe that Jesus was alive without having seen Him with their own eyes?

As the two walked along the dusty road, they talked about Jesus, His sufferings and death. They also talked about the curious reports which were circulating, suggesting He might be alive. *But why did Jesus have to suffer so much?* they wondered. *Why did He have to die? If only He'd become King, as we had hoped.*

Show Illustration #5*

As they were discussing these things, suddenly Someone joined them and walked beside them.

The Stranger asked, "What were you talking about as you walked?"

Cleopas answered, "You must be the only one in Jerusalem who has not heard of the dreadful things which happened in the last few days."

"What things?" asked the Stranger.

"All the things about Jesus of Nazareth," came the reply. "He was a great and powerful Prophet in the things He said and in the miracles He did. But the chief priests and rulers in Jerusalem arrested Him and handed Him over to the Roman government to be condemned to death. And they crucified Him. We had hoped that He had come to set Israel free. But now it's the third day since He was crucified. Some women reported that they were at the tomb early this morning and the body of Jesus was gone. They say they saw angels who told them that Jesus is alive. Some men went to the tomb to check for themselves. They found that it was just as the women had said. The tomb is empty!"

* The Bible does not say that both people were men, though we have pictured them as men. Some believe that Cleopas' companion was his wife. If the Cleopas of John 19:25 is the same as the Cleopas of Luke 24:18, the couple could have been husband and wife.

Then the Stranger said to the two, "How foolish you are! You are so slow to believe in your hearts all that the prophets have written in the Scriptures. It was necessary for Christ first to suffer these things, before He entered into His glory." And then He explained what Moses and the prophets had told about the Messiah who would come and suffer and die. The two listened as this One explained how the Scriptures taught about Jesus and what would happen to Him.

2. JESUS' FRIENDS RECOGNIZE HIM
Mark 16:12-13; Luke 24:28-32

When they reached the village of Emmaus where the two lived, the Stranger turned to go farther. But Cleopas and his companion pleaded with Him, "Please do not go. Come inside and eat with us, and stay with us for the night, for it is getting late." So He accepted their invitation.

Show Illustration #6

It was the custom in Jewish families for the father to give thanks for the food before each meal. But on this occasion the Stranger/Guest picked up a loaf of bread and gave thanks to God for it. Then He broke the bread into pieces and passed it to the others at the table. And suddenly their eyes were opened to recognize the Stranger who was with them. It was Jesus! He really was alive. They could reach right out and . . . no, they could not touch Him. He had disappeared! The place where He had been sitting was vacant. In His risen body, the Lord Jesus was able to appear and disappear in an instant.

The two were amazed. They were not sad now. "Remember how our hearts burned as He talked to us along the way and explained the Scriptures to us?" one said. Now they knew why they felt as they had. Jesus talked with them, and they had not recognized Him.

3. JESUS APPEARS TO HIS DISCIPLES
Luke 24:33-48; John 20:19-23

They rushed to the disciples in Jerusalem. But before they could tell their news, the disciples exclaimed, "The Lord is risen and has appeared to Peter!" Imagine that! The Lord had gone to Peter, the one who had denied Him three times.

Show Illustration #7

Then Cleopas and his companion reported that Jesus appeared to them, was with them in their home, and ate with them.

Suddenly, their joy turned to fear. Jesus Himself stood before them! "Peace be unto you," He said. The doors were still locked. How, then, had Jesus entered? They were terrified, thinking it must be His spirit.

"Why are you afraid?" Jesus asked. "Why are you doubting that it is really I?" He held out His hands. "Look at My hands and My feet. Touch Me and see. A spirit does not have a body of flesh and bones as I have." They looked at His hands and feet. Yes, there were the nail prints. He did have a living body.

Jesus asked, "Do you have anything to eat?" They gave Him a piece of broiled fish. As they watched, He ate it–for He was truly alive! Then Jesus said, "Peace be unto you. As the Father has sent Me, even so I send you." To whom was He sending them? To a world of lost sinners–a world which must hear the good news of the risen Saviour. As God had sent the Lord Jesus to the world, so Jesus sent His disciples. His resurrection power would be their power.

4. THOMAS BELIEVES
John 20:24-29

What a wonderful experience for the disciples! One disciple, Thomas, was not there that evening. Later, when the others told him what happened, he said, "Unless I see for myself the prints of the nails in His hands and put my finger into His side, I shall not believe."

Show Illustration #8

Eight days later the disciples were again together in a room. Again the doors were locked. This time Thomas was present. As before, Jesus suddenly stood among them. "Peace be unto you," He said. Then, turning to Thomas, He commanded, "Look at My hands and put your hand into My side. Do not be without faith any longer. Believe!"

Thomas cried, "My Lord and my God!"

Jesus said, "You have believed because you saw Me. But blessed are those who have not seen Me and yet have believed."

In the next few weeks many of His followers saw Jesus. Once He appeared to a gathering of more than 500 people. (See 1 Corinthians 15:6.) There was no doubt about it–Jesus was alive!

But let me ask you a question. Have you seen Jesus with your eyes? No. You and I have not seen Him. Can we then believe that He is alive? Yes. We believe by faith. Remember what Jesus said to Thomas: "Blessed are those who have not seen Me and yet have believed."

We can have our sins forgiven by committing ourselves to the Lord Jesus. This we do by believing that He is the Son of God who died for us and rose again. All who trust in Him will someday see Jesus even as the disciples saw Him.

Perhaps you already have believed in Christ. But you are a fearful believer, or powerless. Maybe you are a doubtful believer. To the disciples who were fearful, the Lord Jesus said, "Peace be unto you." To the powerless disciples Jesus said, "Peace be unto you. As the Father hath sent Me, even so I send you." To Thomas, the one who doubted that the Lord had risen, Jesus said, "Peace be unto you. Do not be without faith any longer. Believe!" If today you are fearful or powerless or doubtful, Jesus says, "Peace be unto you."

Lesson 3
THE RECOMMISSIONED DISCIPLES

Scripture to be studied: John 21

The *aim* of the lesson: To teach that Jesus wants believers to tell others about Himself.

What your students should *know*: Jesus wants believers to follow Him wholly.

What your students should *feel*: A love for and gratitude to the risen Saviour.

What your students should *do*: Follow Jesus and serve Him with all their hearts.

Lesson outline (for the teacher's and students' notebooks):
1. The disciples wait to see Jesus (John 21:1-3).
2. Jesus comes to the disciples (John 21:4-14).
3. Jesus questions Peter (John 21:15-17).
4. Peter follows Jesus (John 21:18-22).

The verse to be memorized:

That if thou shalt confess with thy mouth the Lord Jesus, and shalt believe in thine heart that God hath raised Him from the dead, thou shalt be saved. (Romans 10:9)

NOTE TO THE TEACHER

Every prophecy concerning the birth, life, death and resurrection of our Lord Jesus Christ was fulfilled precisely as predicted. Through His death and resurrection, forgiveness was made available to every person on earth–excluding no one! What do these wonderful truths mean to you? They should fill you with overwhelming love and gratitude to the risen Saviour. And this love should cause you to want to obey and serve Him, even as He commanded: "Go, tell that I am risen. Feed My sheep."

It should give you great joy to teach the glorious doctrine of the resurrection.

THE LESSON

The news of the resurrection of Jesus brought much joy to His followers. Peter was especially glad that Jesus was alive. He was glad, too, that he had been able to see Jesus three times since the resurrection. Jesus looked the same to Peter, and yet there was something different about Him. He could appear and disappear instantly even though the doors were locked. Peter had seen it happen. Every time Jesus held out His hands, Peter could see the scars from the nails. It doubtless reminded Peter of that dreadful day when he had broken his promise to the Lord Jesus.

Peter remembered how proud and sure of himself he had been when he had promised to be true to Jesus. "Even if all the others forsake You," he had boldly declared, "I shall never forsake You. I am ready to go with You to prison and to death." That was a big promise, and Peter had meant what he said. But now Peter remembered only too well that he had not kept his word. He *had* forsaken Jesus. But worse than that, he had denied three times that he even knew Jesus.

So, although Peter was glad that Jesus was alive, he was still ashamed that he had denied the Lord. He wondered if things could ever be the same again between the two of them. Could Peter dare to call himself a disciple of Jesus now? Would Jesus want Peter to work for Him again? Peter was not sure. He had failed miserably.

1. THE DISCIPLES WAIT TO SEE JESUS
John 21:1-3

After having seen the Lord Jesus three times, Peter still had many troubled thoughts about himself and his past. But he was hopeful. He remembered that Jesus promised to meet the disciples in Galilee. (See Matthew 26:32.)

Show Illustration #9

Peter wanted to see Jesus again, and so did the other disciples. So they went to a favorite place beside the Sea of Galilee. Peter, Thomas, Nathanael, James, John and two other disciples were there. They did not know exactly when Jesus would come. But Peter became tired of waiting. "I'm going fishing," he said.

"We shall go with you," said the other disciples. And they did. It was nighttime, usually a good time to fish. And Peter, James and John were good fishermen. They had done it many times. But on this night, no matter where they rowed their boat on the Sea of Galilee, they could not catch a fish–not even one.

2. JESUS COMES TO THE DISCIPLES
John 21:4-14

All night long they tried. At last the sun began to come up. As the disciples looked toward the shore, they saw a man standing there, but couldn't see who he was. The man called out, "Did you get any fish?"

"No!" they replied.

Show Illustration #10

"Cast your net on the right side of the boat and you will get some," the man assured them.

The disciples wondered how this man could be so sure. But they cast their net over the right side of the boat. And immediately the net was full of fish. It was a miracle. Suddenly John exclaimed, "It is the Lord!"

When Peter heard that, he grabbed his clothes, put them on, jumped into the water, and swam to shore. The other disciples rowed their boat to the place where Jesus and Peter waited for them. They dragged the full net behind the boat.

When they reached the shore, the disciples saw a fire on which were fish and bread. The Lord Jesus knew they would be hungry. "Bring the fish that you have caught," Jesus told them. Peter waded out to the net and pulled it onto land. The net was full of fish–153 big ones! It was really too much for the net to hold without breaking. Yet it did not break. It was another miracle!

"Now come and have breakfast," Jesus invited. Not one of them needed to ask, "Who are You?" for they all recognized their risen Lord. Jesus passed the bread and the fish to each disciple.

3. JESUS QUESTIONS PETER
John 21:15-17

Show Illustration #11

After they had eaten, Jesus turned to Peter and asked, "Peter, son of John, do you deeply love Me?"

"Yes, Lord, You know that I am very fond of You," Peter replied.

Jesus said, "Then feed My lambs; teach My young and tender disciples."

Jesus asked a second time, "Peter, son of John, do you deeply love Me?"

Again Peter responded: "Yes, Lord, You know that I am very fond of You."

Jesus commanded, "Feed, tend My sheep; look after My mature disciples."

The third time Jesus asked, "Peter, son of John, are you fond of Me?"

Peter was grieved at the way Jesus asked the question the third time. But he must answer the One whom he had denied three times. "Lord," he said sadly, "You know everything. You know that I am very fond of You."

Jesus ordered, "Feed, teach My sheep."

Peter knew now that Jesus truly wanted him to be a disciple. He had been forgiven his terrible sin. He could serve the Lord again. Oh, he had much more to learn of real deep love for Jesus, but he would learn that in time to come.

4. PETER FOLLOWS JESUS
John 21:18-22

After questioning Peter, Jesus told him about something that was going to happen in the future. Jesus said, "When you were young you took care of yourself and went where you wanted to go. But when you become old someone else will direct you and take you where you do not want to go." The Lord was explaining how Peter was going to die and how he would glorify God in his death. (It is said that Peter died on a cross when he was old, and that he asked to be crucified upside down, for he did not feel worthy to be crucified as Jesus was.) Peter was going to be different from the kind of man he had been. He would no longer be afraid to suffer and die for the Lord.

Then Jesus said to Peter, "Follow Me."

Show Illustration #12

Peter obeyed immediately. Looking back, he saw that John, the disciple whom Jesus dearly loved, was following too. Peter wondered how John would die. Would he, too, be crucified? So Peter asked Jesus, "What about him, Lord? How will he die?"

Jesus replied, "If I want John to live until I come, that should make no difference to you. You follow Me."

What Jesus said to Peter He says also to us: "Follow Me. Do not be concerned about others. I shall show you what you are to do. You follow Me."

Jesus, the risen Saviour and Lord wants to lead us into paths of service for Him. He will direct us in that service. There are many things that we can do for Him if we follow Him.

Perhaps you have confessed Jesus as your Lord and have believed in your heart that God raised Jesus from the dead. If you have truly done that, you are saved. But are you filled with a deep love for the living Lord, or are you only fond of Him? Are you, like Peter after Christ's resurrection, willing to follow Jesus and serve Him with all of your heart?

Lesson 4
THE RESURRECTION OF OUR LORD

NOTE TO THE TEACHER

The doctrine of the resurrection of the Lord Jesus Christ is vitally important to the believer in Christ, for the Bible teaches that if Christ had not risen, we would have to remain in our sins. (See 1 Corinthians 15:14, 17.) If His body had stayed in the grave, there would be no salvation for sinful mankind.

The resurrection of Jesus Christ proves His deity. It is the very center of the Christian faith. This doctrine is a source of encouragement to the child of God because it assures him of victory in his Christian life. Paul speaks of the "power of His [Christ's] resurrection" (Philippians 3:10). Christians have access to this resurrection power. But many do not avail themselves of all that Christ offers.

Do you know victory in your life by the power of the risen Lord? Let God look into your heart. Only then can you pass this teaching on to others with assurance and confidence.

The *aim* of the lesson: To show that the resurrection of Jesus Christ proves His deity.

What your students should *know*: Because the Lord Jesus died and rose again they can be saved by believing in Him.

What your students should *feel*: A desire to believe in the Lord Jesus.

What your students should *do*: Confess with their mouths the Lord Jesus and believe in their hearts that God has raised Him from the dead.

Lesson outline (for the teacher's and students' notebooks):

1. Many people saw Christ after His resurrection (1 Corinthians 15:4-8).
2. Jesus had a resurrected body (Luke 24:36-43).

3. The importance of the resurrection (John 2:19-22; 14:1-3; Romans 1:4; 4:25).

The verse to be memorized:

That if thou shalt confess with thy mouth the Lord Jesus, and shalt believe in thine heart that God hath raised Him from the dead, thou shalt be saved. (Romans 10:9)

THE LESSON

Do you believe everything you hear? Suppose someone told you that if you were to jump off a high cliff you would not fall. Would you believe it? Suppose someone said to you, "If you flap your arms real fast you will fly like a bird." Would you believe it? Of course not! (If you are not certain, flap your arms and see what happens. But do not try to jump off a cliff!) We should not believe everything we hear.

But if something is true, should we believe it? Yes.

In our last three lessons we have been talking about something that is true–and very important. It is so important that if we believe it, we shall be saved. If we *will* not believe it we *cannot* be saved. Do you remember what that something is? Our memory verse talks about it and says we must believe it to be saved. It is the resurrection of Jesus Christ. We must believe that God raised Jesus from the dead.

Perhaps you are asking, "How do I know for certain that Jesus rose from the dead?" Many people want to know this. That is why God gave us many proofs and witnesses of the resurrection of our Lord.

In one of our recent lessons, I showed you an illustration from this book I hold in my hand. (*Teacher:* Keep *Visualized Bible* closed.) It was a picture of Mary Magdalene at the empty tomb. If you were not present at that session you have only my word for it. But I want one of you who did see the illustration to tell the class that you saw it. You will be a witness to the statement I made. (Teacher, have three or four, one after the other, as witnesses to prove that you did show an illustration of Mary at the empty tomb. Then ask anyone who was absent when the picture was shown whether he now believes the statement, having heard the witnesses. If each witness would give a detail included in the illustration this would give further proof of the truth. Before proceeding with the lesson, show illustration #4.)

1. MANY PEOPLE SAW CHRIST AFTER HIS RESURRECTION
1 Corinthians 15:4-8

The Word of God says: "Now Christ is risen from the dead." (See 1 Corinthians 15:20.) How do we know this is true? Let us call on some Bible witnesses to prove it.

Show Illustration #13A

Here is Peter. (Point to Peter in the illustration.) Listen to what he has to say about the resurrection of Christ Jesus. "Jesus is risen! I saw the empty tomb. But more than that, I saw Jesus Himself. I heard Him speak. I saw Him eat. He told me to feed His sheep. So I am going to tell thousands of people that He died and rose again from the dead." (See John 20:6-7; Luke 24:36-43; John 21:1-25; Acts 2:22-24.)

Now let us ask John. "John, what do you have to say about the resurrection? Did Jesus really rise from the dead?"

Show Illustration #13B

"He most certainly did! I should know. I too saw the tomb empty. But I also saw Jesus in His living body a number of times after that. I saw Him do things no one else could do. I am so sure that He is risen and that everything Jesus has said is true that I have written it down in a book–the Gospel of John. I could have written much more, but there really would not be room in the world for all the books if everything that Jesus did was written down." (See John 20:8, 19, 30, 31; 21:24-25.)

Thank you, John, for that testimony.

Whom shall we call for our next witness? How about Thomas? He was the one, you remember, who was absent when Jesus first appeared to the disciples after the resurrection. "Thomas, what can you tell us about the resurrection of Jesus? Can we really believe that Jesus has risen from the dead even though we have not seen Him?"

Show Illustration #13C

Thomas seems a bit embarrassed as he answers. "Do not be foolish as I was. When some of the other disciples told me Jesus had risen, I did not believe it. I said I would not believe unless I saw Him for myself and could put my fingers into His wounds. How foolish of me! Not long afterwards Jesus suddenly appeared to us as we talked one evening. I saw the nail prints in His hands. I could reach out and touch Him. He was not a spirit. I saw Him in a living body. I do believe He arose from the dead. You can believe it, too, even though you have not seen Him." (See John 20:19-29.)

We have heard what these disciples have to say about the resurrection. Shall we talk next to the Roman soldiers who guarded the tomb? Would they be good witnesses of what happened? No! The soldiers are too frightened to tell the truth. They were warned to lie about the resurrection and say that the disciples stole the body of Jesus. Since they will not tell the truth, we cannot let them give testimony.

But there are others whose testimonies are true and reliable.

Show Illustration #14A

Mary Magdalene who saw Jesus after He had risen has a smile on her face. We can be certain she has the same good news as the disciples. She wants to tell us, "He is risen!" (See Luke 24:10-11.)

Show Illustration #14B

The angel says, "Jesus, who was crucified, is risen." (See Mark 16:5-6.)

Show Illustration #14C

Most important of all, Jesus Himself tells us about His resurrection: "See My hands and My feet, that it is I Myself. Touch Me and see" (Luke 24:39).

What better proof could there be of the resurrection of Jesus Christ than:

1. The empty tomb (Luke 24:3). (Point to it in illustration #14b.)
2. The many witnesses of His appearances: the disciples, Mary Magdalene, other women, two disciples on the road to Emmaus, and others–500 at one time. (See Luke 24:48; 1 Corinthians 15:4-8.)
3. The testimony of Jesus (Luke 24:44).

There are other important truths to be remembered about the resurrection of Jesus Christ. (These should be written in our notebooks.)

2. JESUS HAD A RESURRECTED BODY
Luke 24:36-43

This is important to us because the Bible tells us that someday we are going to be like Him. (See 1 John 3:2; Philippians 3:21.)

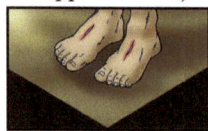

Show Illustration #15A

1. It was a living body, not a spirit. His body had flesh and bones. (See Luke 24:36-43.) His body could be seen. (See John 20:20.) His body had the had the marks of the nails and the spear. (See John 20:24-29.) He was recognizable. (See Luke 24:31.) He could eat. (See Luke 24:41-43.)

Show Illustration #15b

2. His body was different from a natural body. It could pass through locked doors. (See John 20:19.) At times it was not recognizable. (See Luke 24:13-16; John 20:14-15; 21:4, 12; Mark 16:12.) Jesus was able to vanish out of sight. (See Luke 24:31, 51.)

Show Illustration #15C

3. His resurrected body could never die again. (See Romans 6:9-10; Revelation 1:18.) And think of it–someday when we are in beautiful Heaven, we shall be like Him! (The illustration reminds us that Heaven is a place of light. Why? Because the Lord Jesus Himself is the light. See Revelation 21:23.)

3. THE IMPORTANCE OF THE RESURRECTION
John 2:19-22; 14:1-3; Romans 1:4; 4:25

The resurrection is important because:
1. It showed that Jesus really is the Son of God (Romans 1:4).
2. It proved that He told the truth about Himself (John 2:19-22).
3. It fulfilled the prophecies of the Old Testament (Psalm 16:10).
4. It assures the believer that he is accepted with God (Romans 4:25).

Show Illustration #16

5. It assures the believer of his future resurrection and eternal life (John 14:1-3, 19; 2 Corinthians 4:14; 1 Thessalonians 4:14). (The top of the illustration is a reminder of Heaven with its glorious light–where believers in Christ will spend eternity.)
6. It has given us a new day of worship–Sunday, the Lord's day. It is not His birth, nor his death, but His resurrection that is observed every Sunday–the first day of the week.
7. It promises a day of judgment (Acts 17:31). But you do not need to fear if you have believed that Jesus died and rose again. (The fire at the bottom of the illustration is a reminder that those who are not believers in Christ will be judged. See Revelation 20:12-15.)

What does the resurrection of Jesus Christ mean to you? Do you truly believe that He is the Son of God? Have you confessed with your mouth the Lord Jesus and believed in your heart that God has raised Him from the dead? (See Romans 10:9.) If you have, then you are safe. If you have not, you are still dead in your sins. Will you this moment place your trust in the risen Lord Jesus and receive Him as your Saviour? Then you can be a living witness for Him.

www.ingramcontent.com/pod-product-compliance
Lightning Source LLC
Chambersburg PA
CBHW060806090426
42736CB00002B/177